CRAFTY IDEAS WITH GROWING THINGS

Melanie Rice

Illustrated by Lynne Farmer

Photography by Chris Fairclough

HODDER AND STOUGHTON
LONDON SYDNEY AUCKLAND TORONTO

574

**To Chris, Catherine and Alex,
for all their help.**

Note to reader
tbsp = tablespoon
tsp = teaspoon

British Library Cataloguing in Publication Data

Rice, Melanie
    Crafty ideas with growing things.
    1. Children's gardens
    I. Title
    635.083

    ISBN 0-340-52574-6

Text copyright © Melanie Rice 1991
Illustrations copyright © Lynne Farmer 1991

First published 1991

Published by Hodder and Stoughton Children's Books,
a division of Hodder and Stoughton Ltd,
Mill Road, Dunton Green, Sevenoaks, Kent TN13 2YA

Design by Sally Boothroyd

Cover illustration by Lynn Breeze

Book list compiled by Peter Bone, Senior Librarian,
Children's and Schools Services, Hampshire County Library

Printed in Great Britain by BPCC Hazell Books
Paulton, Bristol
Member of BPCC Ltd

CONTENTS

Note to parents and teachers

The activities in this book are meant to be simple and straightforward. Each has been tried out by my own young children at home before being photographed. Every page has clear instructions accompanied by numbered, easy-to-follow illustrations.

You do not need a garden to grow plants: bowls, yoghurt cartons or plant pots, will do just as well. Small peat pots are ideal for growing cuttings and seeds. Generally use potting compost for soil, but bulb fibre when planting crocuses. Indoor plants will need feeding during growing and flowering – use a liquid plant food.

The best indoor environments for growing are sunny window-sills, porches and humid bathrooms but some plants will grow almost anywhere.

Note to children

Things to remember:

1 Read all instructions carefully before you begin so that you know what you have to do. Use the illustrations to help you.

2 Make sure everything you need is ready before you start.

3 Spread newspaper over your working surface to prevent soil rubbing into carpets etc.

4 Clean up any mess when you have finished.

5 Put everything away tidily.

Don't forget to water your plants regularly but avoid drowning them; the soil should be just moist to touch. One final tip – most gardeners will tell you that talking to plants encourages them to grow. Try it and see if you agree.

Melanie Rice

PEBBLE GARDEN

You do not need soil to grow plants. Pebbles and water will do just as well.

You will need:

bowl
busy Lizzie plant
charcoal
pebbles
plant food
sand
scissors
water

1.

1 Put some charcoal in the bottom of the bowl. Then add a layer of sand about 1cm deep and about 4cm of small pebbles.

2 Cut a stalk, about 10cm long from a busy Lizzie.

2.

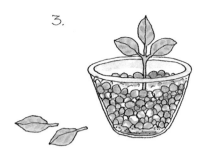

3 Remove the bottom leaves and plant gently in the pebbles.

4 Mix some liquid plant food and water, following the instructions on the bottle. Pour into the bowl just covering the pebbles.

5 Top up with water as the level drops and add plant food monthly.

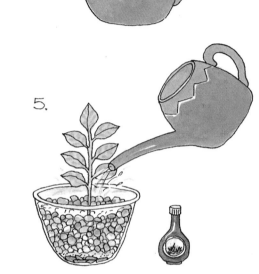

You can also make pebble gardens with ivy and tradescantia.

LAVENDER BAGS

Sweet-smelling lavender bags make lovely presents for friends and family.

You will need:

cotton
cotton material
lavender seeds
needle
pencil
plant pot
plate
potting compost
ribbon
scissors

1.

2.

1 Sow 2 or 3 lavender seeds in compost.

2 Store the pot in a warm place for about 2 weeks, keeping the soil moist.

3 When shoots appear, move the pot to a sunny window-sill.

3.

4 When the lavender has grown, pick a handful of flowers.

5 Draw a circle the size of a plate, on a piece of material and cut it out.

6 Draw a second circle about 2cm inside the first, then sew along the line, using a running stitch.

7 Lay the flowers in the middle of the circle, then pull the thread to gather up the material into a bag.

8 Sew the top to hold the gathers together. Tie a ribbon in a bow round the gathers.

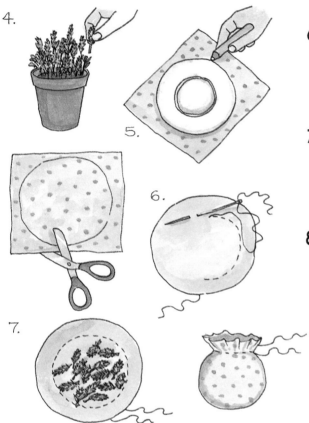

Tubs of lavender can be made from empty margarine boxes, decorated with material.

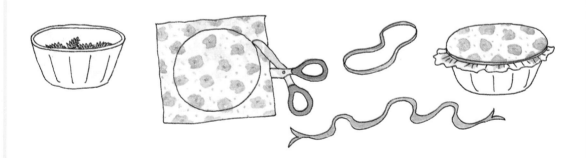

9

TOMATOES

Tomatoes can be grown in pots and are just as tasty as those grown in the garden.

You will need:

garden sticks
peat pot
plant food
plant pot
plastic bag
saucer
soil
tomato plant seeds

1 Soak the peat pot with water then fill with compost. Place the peat pot on a saucer.

2 Place 2 or 3 seeds on top and sprinkle with a thin layer of compost.

3 Wrap loosely in a plastic bag and leave on a window-sill.

4.

4 Remove the plastic when small shoots appear. Keep moist.

5 When the seedlings are 5 to 6cm high, place the peat pot inside a plant pot and top up with soil.

6 Push a stick into the pot to tie the plants upright as they grow.

7 Feed weekly with liquid fertiliser. (Read the instructions on the bottle carefully.)

5.

6.

7.

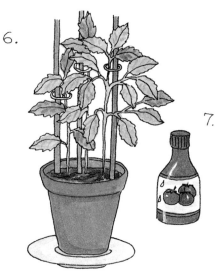

Radishes can be grown in plant pots in the same way.

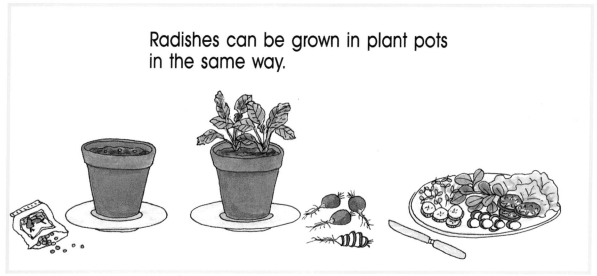

CHRISTMAS CROCUSES

Start growing these bulbs at the end of October and you will have a lovely display of flowers for Christmas and the New Year.

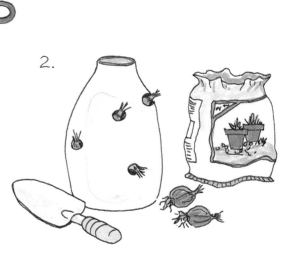

You will need:

bulb fibre
crocus bulbs
plastic soap bottle
scissors
water

1.

2.

1 Cut the top from a plastic soap bottle, then cut holes in the side as shown.

2 Carefully fill the bottle with bulb fibre, planting the bulbs so that their necks peep out from the holes.

3 Gently water the fibre. (Remember to do this over a sink, because water will escape from the holes.)

4 Keep the bottle in a cool dark spot for 4 to 6 weeks or until the shoots are about 4cm long.

5 Bring the bottle out into the light and water again. Keep moist.

6 Turn the bottle round occasionally so all the bulbs get light.

7 When the crocuses finish flowering, cut off the dead stems and plant the bulbs in the garden for next year.

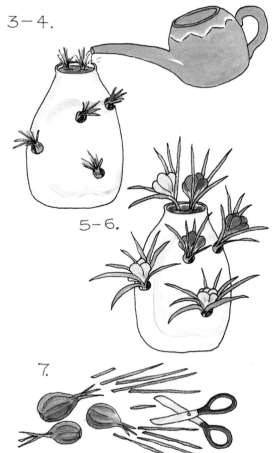

3–4.

5–6.

7.

There are various other bulbs you can grow.

daffodils   hyacinths   tulips

DECORATED POTS

Make your pots as colourful as the plants inside them by creating your own interesting designs.

You will need:

African violet
brush
card or shells
emulsion paint
peat pot
plastic pot
PVA adhesive
scissors
soil
string
white spirit

1 Paint the plant pot with emulsion paint and leave to dry.

2 Paste some glue round the top and bottom, then press lengths of string round the pot on the glue.

3 Stick shells or cut-out cardboard shapes round the middle of the pot and leave to dry.

4 Cut a leaf with a 5cm stem from an African violet. Place in a peat pot with some moist soil.

5 When the new plant grows, cut away the old leaf, then place the peat pot in the decorated pot and top up with soil.

Other ways to brighten up flower pots –

Take some wax rubbings of leaves and arrange them round the sides.

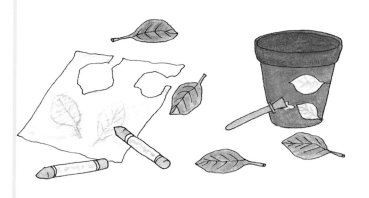

Or, decorate with pictures from magazines.

BOTTLED HERBS

Grow fresh herbs for cooking in your own kitchen garden.

You will need:

charcoal
herb seeds or small plant
pebbles
clear plastic bottle
scissors
soil
400g yoghurt pot

1.

2.

3.

1 Cut the top from a 400g yoghurt container to make a pot about 10cm high.

2 Drop a layer of small pebbles, mixed with a little charcoal, into the bottom of the pot.

3 Pour in the compost to a depth of about 6cm.

4 Either sprinkle a few seeds into the pot and cover with a fine layer of soil, or make a hole in the middle of the soil and gently lower in the plant, pressing the earth firmly round the roots.

5 Water lightly.

6 Cut the bottom off the plastic bottle. Place the bottle over the pot and stand on a sunny window-sill.

7 Lift off the bottle to cut the herbs as you need them.

You can grow whole gardens in bottles.

Choose plants that are small and have pretty leaves. (Avoid flowering plants.) Water only once or twice a year.

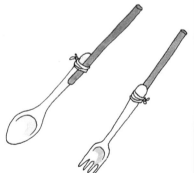

You may need to make special long-handled tools by tying sticks to a spoon and fork, as shown.

MINIATURE GARDEN

Landscape your own garden without going outside.

You will need:

cactus seeds or
    small plants
foil or small mirror
large ice-cream tub
small pebbles
2 plant pots
plastic bag
potting compost

1.

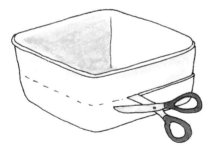

2.

1 Cut a large ice-cream tub to about 4cm high.

2 Place 2 small pots at one end and fill with soil.

3 Lay the piece of foil, or mirror, on the soil, then sprinkle seeds around the edge and in the pots. Water lightly.

3.

4 Sprinkle some tiny stones or shells over the soil, then cover with a plastic bag.

5 Leave for a couple of months in a warm place keeping the soil moist.

6 Remove the plastic when the cactus plants are about 1cm high.

You can also use small ready-grown cacti, but wear rubber gloves when handling them. Gently squeeze the pot so that the roots come out with the earth round them, then pop into a hole in the soil. Press the earth firmly round the roots, then water well.

4 – 5.

6.

You can use any variety of containers for miniature gardens. Plant small flowers such as –

prayer plant

aluminium plant

pansies

maidenhair fern

primrose

small-leafed ivy

African violets

mother of thousands

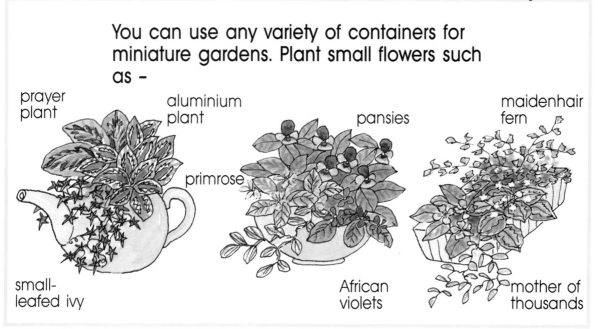

EVERLASTING FLOWERS

These flowers will brighten up your
room all year round.

You will need:

florist's oasis
kitchen ladle
PVA adhesive
scissors
seeds: Everlasting (mixed)
soil
thin string
window box

1.

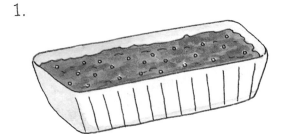

2.

1 Fill window box with soil and
sow several rows of seeds.

2 Cover with a thin layer of soil
and keep moist.

3.

3 As the flowers and grasses
begin to open, cut near the
bottom of the stalks.

4 Tie in bunches and hang upside down in a cool, airy room.

5 Leave to dry for about two months.

6 Cut a piece of florist's oasis to fit the bowl of the ladle and stick down firmly.

7 When the flowers and grasses have dried, cut the stalks shorter and push into the oasis. Arrange with the longer stems at the back and shorter ones at the front until the bowl is full of flowers.

4 – 5.

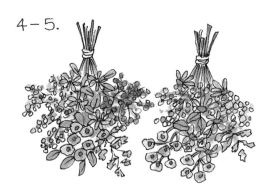

6.

7.

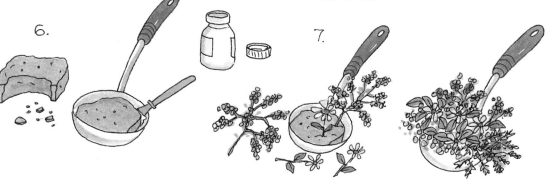

Small baskets, old shoes, even egg-cups can be used as containers for dried flowers.

HAIRY CATERPILLAR

Entertain your guests by serving cress in this amusing hairy caterpillar.

You will need:

card
cotton wool
5 empty egg shells
felt pens
glue
plastic bag
seeds

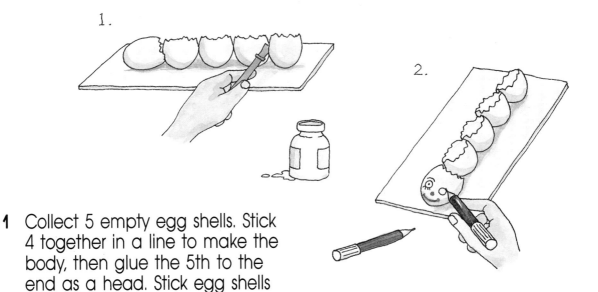

1.

2.

1 Collect 5 empty egg shells. Stick 4 together in a line to make the body, then glue the 5th to the end as a head. Stick egg shells on the card.

2 Paint a face with felt tip pens.

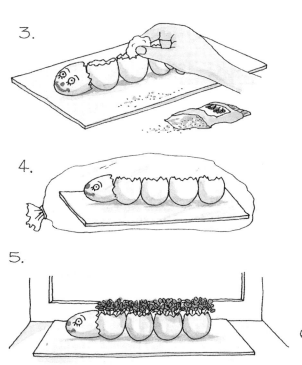

3 Fill the 4 egg shells with damp cotton wool and sprinkle cress seeds thinly on top.

4 Place the caterpillar in a plastic bag and keep in a warm, dark place for two days.

5 Remove the plastic bag and stand on a sunny window-sill for a few more days.

6 Serve for guests to cut and eat with salad or sandwiches.

Growing fruit seeds (they will not produce fruit, but you can grow some very pretty plants).

Collect seeds from –

oranges

apples

lemons

dried dates

peaches

Soak them in water overnight, then plant in yoghurt pots filled with soil. Keep in a warm, dark place for a few weeks.

When shoots appear, place on a sunny window-sill.

HAT PARADE

Create several characters with
different hats and see which
grows the finest.

You will need:

card
carrot
felt pen
glue
pencil
plastic lid
plate
scissors
table tennis ball
wool

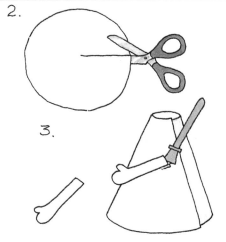

1 Draw round the plate with a
pencil and cut out.

2 Make a cut into the centre of
the circle, then fold into a cone
shape and stick. Cut off the
top.

3 Cut two arm shapes from card
and stick to the sides of the
cone. Use felt pen to colour.

4 Stick a table tennis ball to the top and draw on a face. Add scraps of wool for hair.

5 Stick an up-turned lid to the top of the head.

6 Pour in a little water.

7 Cut 1cm from the top of a carrot and place in the water.

8 Top up the water daily and watch the hat grow.

Try the tops of other root vegetables to make different styles of hat.

beetroot   turnip   parsnip

NASTURTIUM SALAD

The leaves, stems, flowers and seeds of nasturtiums can all be used to make a delicious spicy salad.

You will need:

large bowl	plant pot
small bowl	1 boiled potato
cream	salt
fork	saucer
knife	soil
lettuce	sugar
mustard	teaspoon
powder	vinegar
nasturtium	
seeds	

To make a salad from the crop of nasturtiums:

1 Wash the lettuce and place in a large bowl.

a Fill a pot with soil and sow a few seeds about ½cm deep.

2 Cut 5 nasturtium stalks and leaves and chop into the bowl.

b Place the pot in a warm sunny spot and keep well watered.

3 Slice the potato and mix with the leaves.

4 Lay the nasturtium flowers on top.

5 Mix together in a small bowl:
4 tbsps cream
1 tsp mustard powder
a few chopped nasturtium seeds
$\frac{1}{4}$ tsp salt
$\frac{1}{2}$ tsp sugar
2 tbsps vinegar

6 Pour the mixture over the salad.

Beansprouts are also tasty in salads.

Place a handful of mung beans in a jar. Cover with warm water and leave overnight.

Place a piece of muslin over the top and hold in place with an elastic band. Drain off the water and leave on a sunny window-sill.

Rinse the beans morning and evening for about 1 week.

SPIDER IN A CHAIR

Novelty plant pot holders are fun to make and attractive to look at. Try making this chair for a spider plant to sit in.

You will need:

30 wooden ice-lolly sticks
plant pot
PVA adhesive or glue
saucer or plastic lid
scissors
soil
spider plant

1.

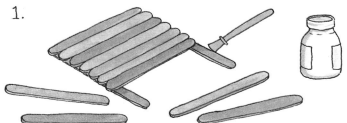

2.

1 Lay 2 lolly sticks on the table and glue 11 sticks across them as shown.

3.

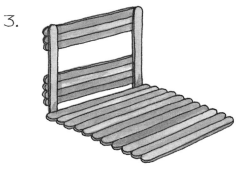

2 Lay 2 more on the table. Glue 7 sticks across them and leave to dry.

3 Glue the pieces together to make the seat and back of the chair.

4 Take another stick and cut in half. Glue each piece upright on the end of the seat as shown. Then glue 2 sticks joining the top of the upright to the middle of the back.

5 Glue 2 more sticks to the uprights and 2 to the back to make legs. Leave to dry.

6 Take a piece from a spider plant and place in the middle of a small pot of soil.

7 Stand on a saucer on the seat of the chair and water well.

Sticks of all shapes and sizes can be used to make frames for plants.

BOOK LIST

If you would like to find out more about plants and how they grow then the following books will help. Your local library should be able to get copies for you.

Coldrey, Jennifer and Bernard, George.
HYACINTH.
A. & C. Black, 1989.　　　*0713630957*
With excellent photographs and cut-away views this book from the *Stopwatch* series shows how the hyacinth grows from bulb to flower.

Eccleshare, Julia.
HERBS AND SPICES.
Hamish Hamilton, 1989.　　*0241124700*
A simple introduction to eleven herbs, which describes how and where they usually grow.

Muller, Gerda.
A GARDEN IN THE CITY.
Macdonald, 1989.　　　*0356168255*
The story of how Ben and Caroline grow things in the garden of their new house. Many gardening ideas and hints.

Parker, Philip.
THE LIFE CYCLE OF A SUNFLOWER.
Wayland, 1988.　　　*1852103086*
After showing how the sunflower develops the book gives some idea of how to grow one yourself.

Tarsky, Sue.
THE WINDOW BOX BOOK.
Methuen/Walker, 1980.　　*0416891101*
All types of window boxes are depicted with clear instructions. Adult help may be needed to set up the box but it will then be a place to grow all kinds of fruit, vegetables or herbs.

Watts, Barrie.
TOMATO.
A. & C. Black, 1989.　　　*071363166X*
Vivid colour photographs show how a tomato plant develops. This is another in the *Stopwatch* series.
Other titles in the series are **Potato, Strawberry, Broad bean** and **Dandelion.**

INDEX